PATCHWORK
STORIES, POEMS,
AND MEDITATIONS
FOR MOTHERS

Patchwork

Stories
Poems
&
Meditations
for
MOTHERS

LIFEJOURNEY
BOOKS

David C. Cook Publishing Co.

David C. Cook Publishing Co., Elgin, Illinois 60120
David C. Cook Publishing Co., Weston, Ontario
Nova Distribution, Ltd., Torquay, England

PATCHWORK
STORIES, POEMS, AND MEDITATIONS FOR MOTHERS
©1987 by David C. Cook Publishing Co.

Edited by Julie Smith
Cover design by Dawn Lauck
Interior design by Dwight Walles

Third Printing, 1991
Printed in Singapore
94 93 92   5 4 3

Library of Congress Cataloging-in-Publication Data
Patchwork: stories, poems, and meditations for mothers.
1. Mothers—Religious life. 2. Mothers—Prayer-books and devotions—English.
BV4529.P37 1987 242'.6431 86-24389

*A woman who fears
the Lord is to
be praised.*

Proverbs 31:30b

Praisingly Yours

Elva McAllaster

> "Praise the Lord, O my soul, and forget not all his benefits." Ps. 103:2

Praisingly Yours, my Father.
Praising You for the mosaic of joy
This day has known, this week has seen.

Light glowing from a tall gold pillar-candle
Through twilight quietudes.
Lovely, lovely.
(And twenty-five cents for that candle
At a yard sale yesterday;
Are You smiling at me, with me?)

Sunrise this morning:
Glinting, reaching, flaming
Praise.

A blue jay, winging
His feathered strong doxologies.

Veined patterns in geranium leaves
Against white curtains.
The lilt and tang of geranium fragrance.

Clouds, dazzle-white,
Becoming very anthems.
Maple boughs and elm tree boles
Each echoing, "Amen, Amen."

A letter from Germany, a letter from Chicago.
A gracious voice from Maryland
Brought to my home by supple wires.

Toothpaste. Trumpets. Frozen blueberries.
A toddler's trustful smiles and movements.
A teen's quick grace.in greeting adults.

News: a weary friend has entered Your Forever.
News: You love me, love me, love me.

Praisingly Yours, my Father.
Praising You for the mosaic of joy
This day has known, this week has seen.

Ma's Busy Day

Arleta Richardson

GRANDMA'S QUILT was almost finished.

"I'd like a dress like this, Grandma," I said, pointing to a square with tiny green leaves and flowers. "This is pretty."

"Yes," replied Grandma. "That was pretty made up. It was one of Ma's dresses, then she made it into an apron. In fact, a lot of these squares came from Ma's aprons. She was never seen anyplace but in church without an apron on."

Grandma laughed. "Pa never let her forget that she tied an apron over her nightgown one night before she got into bed! I remember another day that Ma didn't live down for a long time, too."

Grandma sat down by the table, and I pulled up the kitchen stool.

"When Ma dressed in the morning," Grandma began, "she put on a clean apron over her housedress. Then she carried a fresh one with her to the kitchen to hang on the back door. This was to make sure that, should we have company, there would be a clean apron in close reach and she would be ready to greet the visitor.

"This morning as usual, Ma hung her extra apron on the door and prepared to fix breakfast. I was setting the table and the boys were coming from the barn with the milk. Ma hurried to open the door and let them in. Pep, our big dog, had also seen them coming and figured this might be a chance to get into the warm kitchen. He lunged for the door just as Roy was going through. One of the milk pails flew into the air, and Roy and Pep were covered with fresh warm milk.

" 'Oh, that dog,' Ma sputtered. ''There's only one thing he can do better than make a mess, and that's eat.'

"She mopped up the milk, sent Roy to change his clothes, and rubbed at the front of her apron with a towel.

" 'I haven't time to change now,' she said, and she grabbed the apron from the door and put it on over the spattered one.

"This was baking day, and Ma was busy making bread, pies and cakes, keeping the stove hot, and cleaning up the kitchen. She had no time to think again about her apron. Shortly before dinner time at noon, Ma saw a buggy turn in the lane.

" 'Mabel,' Ma called to me, 'run and get me a fresh apron, will you? Someone is coming up the lane.'

"I brought the apron, and Ma quickly put it on and tied it just as the visitor approached the house. It was a neighbor to ask Ma if she could come that afternoon to see his wife, who was not feeling too well. Of course Ma could, but wouldn't he stay and have dinner with us first?

"After dinner, when Pa and the boys returned to the field, Ma and I packed a basket to take to the neighbor. As we were about to set out, Ma looked down at her apron.

" 'Mabel,' she said, 'I believe I'd better have a fresh apron before we leave.'

"I got another apron and Ma tied it on as we walked to the buggy.

"It was getting on toward suppertime when we returned. Ma planned what we would fix, and we hurried about the kitchen getting supper on the table before Pa and the boys should come in.

"As we prepared to sit down, Ma decided that her apron didn't look very good, so she hurried to the bedroom for another.

"Pa came in and sat down at the table. He watched Ma as she finished taking up the food and supervising the boys' washing.

" 'Maryanne,' Pa said, 'have you been putting on weight?'

" 'Why, no,' Ma replied. 'I don't think so. My clothes feel the same. Why?'

" 'Well,' said Pa, 'I declare you look bigger than you did this morning when I left the house.'

" 'I know why,' I said. 'Ma's got more clothes on than she did this morning.'

"Ma looked puzzled for a moment, then she began to laugh.

" 'I guess I have,' she said. 'I've been rushing around so fast today, I haven't had time to take one apron off before I put the other one on.'

"She began to untie the aprons and take them off. With each one Pa and the boys laughed harder. When finally she had gotten down to the original milk-spattered apron, Ma was laughing as hard as the rest of us.

" 'If we couldn't remember what happened all day any other way,' Pa said when he could speak again, 'we could always count on Ma's aprons to bring us up to date!'

"Ma enjoyed the joke, but she declared that she was going to be presentable if it did take five aprons a day to do it —and one on top of the other, too!"

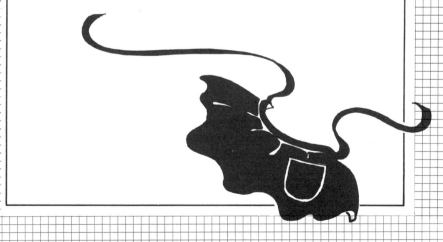

Jeanne Zornes Those Pink

A dirty pair of white tennis shoes almost kicked me into the Slough of Despond the other day.

Usually my husband wore them to the physical education classes he teaches. But after a muddy stint behind the garden Rototiller, they'd been banned to the back porch. The day the "dark" wash could handle a little more, I tossed them in.

Wash over, they emerged. *Pink.*

My new pair of red pants had shared its dyes. Panicked, I tossed the shoes in the next wash load of diapers. Bleach and hot water paled the shoes, but they still looked fit for the decor in our baby Inga's room.

Hastily I stashed the footwear in the back of our closet. But the next morning, as my husband bounced into the kitchen for breakfast, he called out in a mock soprano, "Hey, Tweetie, looky my new tennies!"

That did it. Crying in the sink. A lot of things had piled up too high.

I'd been harboring heaviness over other people's hurts. My prayer list included friends and relatives without jobs; an alcoholic; a woman about to deliver a child her husband didn't want; someone close with a baffling health problem; a friend's runaway son.

Added to that was physical exhaustion. Both our babies had bad colds. For nights, I'd been up and down, up and down, caring for coughs and crying.

Capping it off were little crises destroying my somewhat-organized homemaking. Weary from the fractured nights with sick babies, I'd yielded to the blankets rather than the 6:30 a.m. buzz. At 7:15, the diaper duo began another wake-up chorus. Grabbing the songsters, I dashed toward inventing the quickest-breakfast-yet for my husband.

Right away I noticed ants homesteading the real estate under toddler Zach's high chair. Then Inga wailed about her sore gums and insisted on Mama's comfort.

As one foot patted the life out of ants, and one arm con-soled the baby, my free hand reached inside the refrigerator for eggs. Two played Humpty-Dumpty and nose-dived with a big splat.

Then the pink tennies entered. I'd ruined (at least for color) his best pair of "work" shoes.

Laundry Blues

Like it or not, there are days when molehills become mountains and tennies overrun me like armored trucks. I'm ready to collapse right under the prophet Elijah's juniper tree (I Kings 19) and whine. When I do, I've learned the Great Physician has an Rx for depression that works as well for me as it did for Elijah.

Physical renewal. Worn out from his journeys, ministries, and confrontation with the priests of Baal, Elijah got shut-eye and a catered breakfast on the rocks. On Blue-Pink Tennies Day, I threw away my "must-do" list and yielded to a nap with the babies.

A reminder of God's power and love. Elijah witnesses a great earthquake, windstorm, and fire, then heard the message of a whisper. I got healing whispers from Scripture. And I had a purging prayer time.

An assignment. Elijah was told to anoint two kings and his own sucessor. I had no kings to crown, but a castle to maintain. So a neglected drawer got tidied. Some work jeans got mended and sentenced to the washer. Then I wrestled on the floor with the babies until their laughter turned to hiccups.

Now I realize pink tennis shoes are minor league problems. A few years ago I experienced overwhelming discouragement and grief. Age 31 and still single, I buried both parents within six months. I struggeld with self-esteem, faced joblessness, and endured stress-related health problems.

That's when my Bible study introduced me to Elijah's ways of coping with depression. I learned how God never abandons me. I learned to look up to my new destination in God's grace — to the hills, "From whence cometh my help. My help cometh from the Lord, which made heaven and earth" (Ps. 121:1, 2).

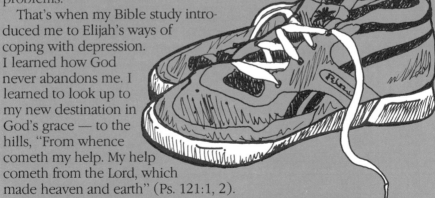

That's true for crises as well as those days the blues creep in with the ants, eggs, and pink tennis shoes.

Do It Again, God!

Carole M. Sherman

At the onset of spring thunderstorms one year, I wondererd just what reaction my friend's three-year-old son would have to them. His parents had tried to explain in advance that lightning and thunder go with rain and that they were all important parts of God's plan for our world. One night a storm hit, a really loud one. They went into the boy's room to see if he needed some reassurance. They found him sitting up in bed watching the storm through his window. Lightning flashed; thunder rolled. Rob clapped his hands, and he said, "Good one! Do it again, God!"

Wouldn't it be great if we could get as excited over seeing the handiwork of God in people's lives as we do at seeing His handiwork in nature? He redeems a sinner; transforms the person's life; gives him a sense of purpose and a new set of values. We ought to be shouting, "Good one! Do it again, God!"

God has wrought many wonders in our lives. What's more, He will do so again and again. That is just too much to keep still about.

Lord, don't let me overlook Your handiwork in my life and in the lives of my friends.

Forgive My Prayers

Lillian Cantleberry

Father,
forgive my rote prayers,
too often centered on self,
petitions for here and now
and "happily ever after."

Forgive my hurried prayers,
trite words
unthinkly said —
a list stamped "Amen."

Forgive my prayers,
Father.

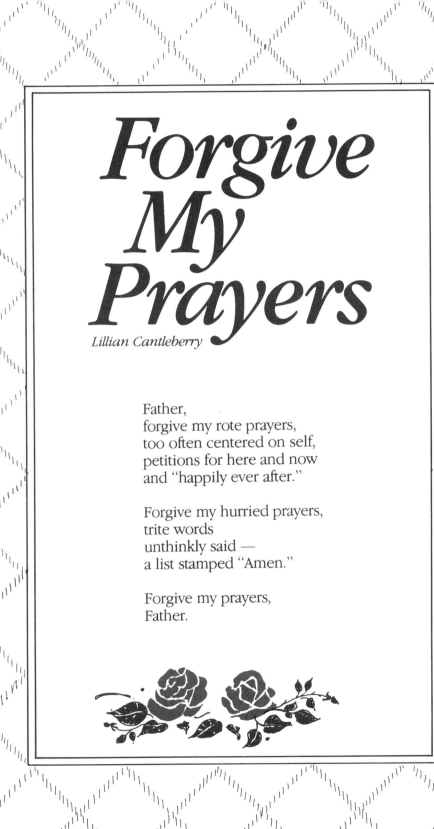

Take a
Midget
Tim Hansel
Vacation

Midget vacations open our eyes to all that we have at our feet, right in our own home. It might include trying to go outside every morning for a week and see something you've never seen before. Just because you've lived in the same house for twenty years doesn't mean you've seen everything.

Here are some other "morning midgets" you might want to try.

- Praise God for the sunrise (that means you have to be up to see it).
- Don't get out of bed until you can think of one thing you're thankful for, and secondly, say, "This is the day that the Lord has made, let us rejoice and be glad" (and really mean it).
- Go outside and yell (as loud as your inhibitions will allow), "Life, I love you!"
- Hug something or someone.
- Instead of saying your normal grace before breakfast, either (a) sing a song, (b) whistle, (c) clap, or (d) just stomp

your feet. In other words, praise him with your whole body, instead of just your lips.

- Phone somebody and wish them a happy day.
- Laugh at least once by the time breakfast is over.
- Be happy by eight o'clock. In other words, refuse to be controlled by your circumstances.
- Do something special for yourself in the morning — make yourself a special cup of tea, kiss your husband, pat your dog, read a favorite section of Scripture. In other words, help yourself set the pace for the day.
- Smile at that face in the mirror and say, "I love you" (if you can't say that, then say, "Jesus loves you," because that's certainly true).
- Tell each member of your family one reason why you're glad they're in your family.
- Tell Jesus one reason why you're glad he's your Lord.
- Think of five reasons you're glad that you're you, i.e., five things you like about yourself, and thank God for them.
- Make it a point to meet someone new before lunchtime. You never know what might happen.

Shirley Pope Waite

Spiritual Assets

My 90-year-old friend is in a nursing home. Her hearing has been poor for years, but she enjoys handwork, reading, and watching television. Now her eyes are failing, and these simple pleasures are also denied her. Yet for the most part, she remains cheerful.

One day I asked her about it.

"Well, dear, I just go to the bank more these days." Was my friend confused? She must have seen my puzzled look.

Pointing to her forehead, she said, "This bank — the storehouse. I dredge up old memories — the good ones, of course — but they're only the interest that has been accumulating in my bank. And my, many of them are interesting!"

She paused, as if recalling an old joy.

"Then I turn to the principal — the old Sunday school songs, the hymns, and best of all, the Scriptures I've memorized. They're the principal items in my bank. The Bible says, 'Thy word have I hid in mine heart . . .' but here is where I've really hidden it." She again tapped her head.

Leaning back on her pillow, she looked at me intently through her thick-rimmed glasses. "Interest or principal — I draw out any amount I want. But there's always an ample supply the next time I make a trip to my mental bank."

She reached for the well-worn leather Bible on her nightstand. Handing it to me, she said, "I sometimes get discouraged. Then I remember Isaiah 46:4. Read it to me, will you?"

I turned to the underlined passage: ". . . even to your old age I am He, and to gray hairs I will carry you. I have made, and I will bear; I will carry and will save."

On my way home, I wondered about my own spiritual assets. What positive, happy memories did I have for interest? How about God's Word as the principal resource in my mental bank? In this day of financial upheaval, I knew that these possessions are the greatest investment for my future.

Another Comforter

Arliss Benham

Overnight visits to Grandma's house were a whole new world — Grandma turning the crank on the butter churn; kneading yeasty, homemade bread; ironing on a board placed between two chairs with a flatiron heated on the old wood stove.

Then bedtime came with the long trek up the stairs, strange noises, dark shadows. But Grandma would always say, "There's an extra comforter on the foot of the bed."

What a haven! Just pull that comforter up over my head and strange noises were shut out, lurking shadows disappeared, no bright flashes of lightning could be seen, no cold chill could penetrate its warmth. But most of all, every hand-stitched piece of that comforter radiated Grandma's love and care.

And Grandma reminds me of God. Not only did He send His Son for our redemption — He went one step beyond and sent "another Comforter" — a haven for every need, shelter for every storm, light for our darkest days, healer of our deepest sorrows, and the warmth of His very own love.

Oh, God I find peace in Your Comforter.

Necessities of Life

Nora Ann Kuehn

I gave the faded jeans another careful inspection. I hadn't missed any rips, but there were some dangerously thin spots. No wonder nine-year-old Jimmy had tested their seat strength the other evening in front of the full-length mirror.

Threadbare clothes were just one reason why I felt guilty about hanging on to our two acres after my husband's death. There was the matter of the new bike Mrs. Larson had bought her son David. How Jimmy's eyes had lighted up when he told me about it!

Mrs. Larson was only an acquaintance, but I knew her son like my very own. He spent more time at our house than he did his own. He and Jimmy were closer than paste and wallpaper.

The door slammed, announcing Jimmy's arrival from school. "Lord, please show me how to give my son the real necessities of life," I prayed as I went downstairs.

Jimmy was helping himself to the chocolate cake I had baked that morning, "How was school today?" I asked, replacing the cake cover.

"All right," he replied, slipping onto the kitchen stool and stuffing his mouth with cake. I was surprised when he suddenly said, "Let's go horseback riding."

"You know I can't ride a horse," I answered. "Why didn't you bring David to go with you?"

"He's out riding his new bike," Jimmy replied as he studied the scuffed toe of his boot.

My heart raced, I had asked God for a sign. Was this shabby, disappointed boy my answer. Well, tomorrow I would list the place for sale and apply for a job in town.

Jimmy's coaxing interrupted my thoughts. 'Come on, Mom, I'll show you how to ride Old Pard," he grinned at me. "You won't fall off because Old Pard won't move that fast."

I grasped for an excuse, but could find no real reason not to go. "Well, go bridle the horses," I said reluctantly. "When you get your mind set on something, it's easier to agree with you."

He jumped off the stool and planted one of his rare, shy kisses on my cheek. "Mom, you're swell."

"I wish we had a saddle," I said, recalling that once, when I was a very small girl, I sat on a horse while my father led it around the yard. The only part of the ride I trusted was clinging to the saddle horn.

Jimmy, already loping down the path, stopped to call back, "Don't be chicken, Mom. Anyway, it's easier to ride bareback."

I brushed up the cake crumbs, then pulled on one of my husband's old shirts. "The things I do to please your son," I whispered past the lump in my throat. For a second the shirt seemed to hang like a hug around my shoulders. I heard

Jimmy coming up the lane with the horses, and brushed a sleeve across my tear-filled eyes and went out the door.

Jimmy tied his horse to the fence and led Old Pard over to me.

"How will I ever get on?" I asked.

"Like this," Jimmy said, grabbing a handful of mane and swinging himself up. He slipped off and waited for me to follow his example.

With quaking knees and gritted teeth, I grabbed a handful of the horse's coarse mane and gave what I thought was a terrific leap. My feet came only a few inches off the ground. Out of the corner of my eye I saw Jimmy, bent double with laughter.

I scowled at him. "What's so funny?"

Jimmy sobered. "Here, let me boost you up." He grabbed me around the knees and gave a heave that sent me almost over the horse's back. I hung like a sack of meal, my hands closer to the ground than my feet.

"Sit up!" Jimmy yelled.

"I can't," I screamed. "I'm too far over." I felt myself slipping and dug my knees into the horse's sides for balance. That was a mistake; Old Pard took it as a signal to move on. I could see the ground coming up to meet me.

"Jimmy!" I shouted. "I'm falling. Quick, drag me back."

There was a firm grip on my ankles and a mighty jerk. Jimmy and I hit the ground together. "Are you hurt?" I asked when I had enough breath.

"No," he answered. "We just need a derrick to get you on the horse."

"Well, you can't say I didn't try," I said, getting up and brushing the dust from my jeans.

"I got it!" Jimmy said, jumping to his feet. "Climb up on the fence, Mom. Then you can step right over the horse's back."

Gingerly, I climbed up on the fence and Jimmy led Old Pard alongside. Teetering dangerously, I extended one leg. When it was almost over, I discovered it was the wrong leg. By the time I got that one back and the other foot off the fence, Old Pard had moved over. I was forced to get both feet back on the fence in a hurry or fall on my face in the dust.

Jimmy pursed his lips and shook his head. "I'll stand in front of the horse so he can't move," he said, leading Old Pard back to the fence. "And, Mom, don't take so long to get on this time!"

Old Pard was in position with Jimmy's young shoulder planted against him. Shakily, I stretched my leg out, and this time I landed on the horse's back with a jarring whack.

Jimmy sighed and swung onto his mount. The horses set off at a brisk trot that kept me bouncing like a rubber ball. In time, Jimmy looked back. Seeing my plight, he slowed his horse to a walk. I was happy to see that Old Pard was willing to follow suit.

The new pace was much better, and I was soon able to relax a little. The sun was going down. A cool breeze came up and fanned my hot brow. I looked at my son's happy face, and a feeling of peace stole over me.

"Mom," he said, "do you know that we've already ridden a mile?"

I laughed. "Better make mine two. I've gone your mile and

another one up and down."

He chuckled. "Mom, you're keen."

Back at the gate he gave me a hug when I tumbled off into his arms.

"Don't you just love living out here in the country?" he asked.

"You can have a lot more when I sell the place and get a job," I said, leaning my cheek against his sun-streaked hair.

"I don't want you to ever do that," he said quickly.

"I could buy you a bike like David's if I had a job," I pointed out.

He flashed me a grin. "Mom, watching you get on a horse is more fun than riding David's bike. Can David go with us next time?"

At the mention of a next time, I groaned but said bravely, "I don't see why not."

He gave me another hug. "I know one thing for sure," he said.

"What's that, I asked happily.

"David would give his new bike any day to have his mom spend more time with him. She's always busy working or going places with friends."

I looked closely at his serious young face. "Did David tell you that?"

"Sure. The reason his mother got him that new bike was to keep him home. She thinks he bothers you coming over here so often."

"You tell David he's no bother," I said firmly. Then with my legs still contoured to Old Pard's sides, I walked toward the house.

Suddenly, I realized the truth of what the Bible teaches about material things.

Nothing is more important than caring and being there for those you love. Without knowing it, I was giving my son the real necessities of life.

FROM A
Mother's Journal

Bonnie Wheeler

Dennis is reading from Proverbs 31. I begin to squirm as I compare myself to this virtuous woman.

I fear that the words from my mouth are seldom full of wisdom.

There are days when I have trouble getting my children to even "rise up," much less call me blessed.

My family is more apt to be clothed in hand-me-down denims than threads of scarlet.

The gas and electric company have just raised their rates again and I fear for the snow.

As for the marketplace . . . I must admit that I spend, not sell.

And my candle flickereth out in early evening.

Dennis smiles as he finishes and the children bring me treasures . . .

- a plastic heart, oven baked and slightly warped, "for you to wear to church, Mommy."

- a card glopped with glitter because Melissa likes the way it feels.

- a breadboard lovingly, if unevenly, held together with a year's supply of Elmer's glue.

- and an omelet, "just the way you like it," burned and crunchy.

Virtuous woman, Lord? No . . . but they love me anyway.

Final Scene

Evelyn Minshull

Lord,
how I yearn for
thunderclap denouements,
   for You to stride
   from the wings
     (third act,
     final scene)
   and set things straight,
     resoundingly
   to say, "Take that!"
     to my enemies —
     to one who threatens my child,
     to the detractors of my friends
     and those who distort directions
       in the work I love,
     to those who
       (anywhere)
     damage with hatred and hostility.

But
Your ways
   (fortunately)
are not mine.
Nor do I even desire such drama
when —
in some certain scene
I am cast
   as villain.

All Through the Night

Sleep, my babe, lie still and slumber,
All through the night,
Guardian angels God will lend thee,
All through the night;
Soft, the drowsy hours are creeping,
Hill and vale in slumber sleeping
Mother, dear, her watch is keeping,
All through the night.

Thoughts from the Psalms

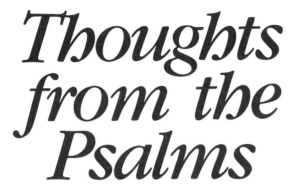

Elspeth Murphy

You know what, God?
Sometimes when I'm sad,
I close my eyes
and pretend I'm
a little baby again.
   And then I imagine
that you are a strong
and gentle father,
holding me close to you.
   "There, there," I seem to hear you say.
"Be still now,
and just remember
that I'm your God."

Moments
Remembered

Jeanette Gilge

Before she heard Papa fix the fires Thursday morning, Ellen was awake wishing she never had to swallow again. She came downstairs with a quilt wrapped around her and huddled in a shivering lump on the oven door till Mama came out of the bedroom tying her apron strings.

"You've got a fever all right," Mama said, feeling Ellen's forehead. "Anything hurt?"

"My throat, and I ache all over," Ellen croaked.

"Oh, dear. I sure didn't want you to get sick. Gargle warm salt water and I'll get the goose grease. Nothing better than goose grease rubbed in good and covered with a nice warm woolen cloth. Minnie! Bring down Ella's pillow so she can lie right here on the couch where it's nice and warm."

Even with the little ones yelling and playing around her, Ellen slept occasionally. At noon she ate some chicken soup and drank hot tea and dozed again.

When she woke Mama looked up from the overalls she was patching and smiled — not her everyday smile — a special warm one. Mama had a way of combining a nod, a wink and a smile that made Ellen feel good all over. Ellen could count the times she had seen it, but when she did her heart felt like butter left in the warming oven.

She beamed back an equally affectionate smile.

"Feeling any better?"

Ellen nodded.

"Was hoping you'd wake up. Gets lonesome with no one to talk to but the little ones." She gestured toward the bedroom. "They're sound asleep." She bit off the thread and held the needle toward the light to rethread it.

"Just think. If we were rich you'd never have to patch

overalls. Wouldn't you like to be rich?"

"Can't say I'd miss patching overalls, but I wouldn't like to be rich."

Ellen sat up so fast her head spun. "You wouldn't want to be rich?"

"Oh, I wouldn't mind having more money so you children could go on to school if you wanted to, and we do need a bigger house already, and it would be nice to have an organ so you girls could learn to play — but don't ever think that money alone makes people happy. It takes a lot more than that." She shook the needle at Ellen. "Look at the people who jump out of windows or shoot each other. Those people aren't all poor, you know."

"I s'pose not. But did you ever really know any rich people?"

"Can't say I have. What I learned about them was from reading and from your Aunt Gustie — Papa's sister Gustie, not mine. She worked for wealthy people in Milwaukee." Mama clucked her tongue. "The things she used to tell us!"

"Do you really mean you'd rather be the way we are now than have people do your work and have lots of money?"

"I told you," Mama said, sounding a little aggravated, "I'm happy being me — right here — right now." She put her patching aside and stuck wood in both stoves. "Want some tea? The *Kafee Kuchen* is cool."

"My stomach says 'yes' but my throat says 'no.' " Ellen grinned. "My stomach just won."

Cuddled in Mama's old flannel wrapper, Ellen watched Mama slice fresh cinnamon-topped *Kaffee Kuchen* and pour tea.

It felt good to be at peace with Mama. It was so nice when they could talk like friends.

Reliable Safekeeping

Dale Younce

My neighbors' house burned the week before Christmas. It was tragic; they lost everything. The next day, walking dejectedly through the charred remains attempting to salvage whatever they could, Kurt, the couple's five-year-old, was particularly intent about looking for his "treasure box."

This little box contained all Kurt's choice possessions: coins, buttons, a magnifying glass, a matchbox, and other odds and ends. To him, these were especially valuable. He took great pride in the contents of his treasure box and had kept it hidden so it would be safe.

Kurt found his all-important prize that day exactly where he had hidden it the day before the fire — under a cast-iron frying pan beneath the kitchen sink. And sure enough, the fire had not harmed his treasures.

You and I are God's treasures. We are valuable and precious to Him; He has told us so in His Word. God preserves His treasures and keeps us by His power.

Father, thank You for those special times of keeping that I know about, and also for those only You know of.

Psalms

for
Moms

Marlene Bagnull

Lord, I've just come home from shopping feeling
    disheartened,
        frustrated,
            and exhausted.
Never again will I take my three children with me —
    especially my three-year-old.
I felt so embarrassed by his behavior.
    and even more so by my inability to control him.
And the two others —
    who are older and should know better —
        only encouraged his naughtiness.
Lord, why am I so ineffective
    in getting my children to obey me?
Please give me the wisdom I need.
Help me to walk more closely with You —
    to observe Your ways of
        training and disciplining.
Show me how I need to grow in obedience to You
    that, in turn, I might know how
        to nurture an obedient spirit within my children.

Beatitudes for Parents of Grown Children

Win Couchman

Blessed are the parents of grown children who encourage their children more than they criticize them. For this attitude will lift their children's burdens.

Blessed are the parents of grown children who do not have all their social eggs in the basket of their children. For when the children move away, the parents will not be impossibly lonely.

Blessed are the parents of grown children who welcome daughters and sons-in-law. For they will be freshened by new ideas, traditions, and interests. Indeed, their hearts and minds will be enlarged.

Blessed are the parents of grown children who do not interfere in the raising of the grandchildren. For the children and grandchildren can then become their permanent friends.

Blessed are the parents of grown children who let them find a way in their relationships with siblings. For the children will appreciate the freedom to know one another as adults.

Blessed are the parents of grown children who pray for them daily, love them intensely, and help them when it's appropriate.

Blessed are the parents of grown children who depend on God's Spirit. For they, themselves, will be blessed.

Enough Is More Than Enough

Tim Hansel

Enough is enough—if not more than enough. If I can be satisfied with little, then enough becomes a banquet. Peace is both a process of panting after God's own heart, and also letting him find you. Because you are found, you are free to seek. And you find that the God at the end of the journey is the same one you knew at the beginning. Learning to let life happen rediscovers the importance of small things. It relishes childlike joys of the everyday wonders of being alive. "Yet they seek me daily and delight to know my ways" (Isa. 58:2).

Some of God's miracles are small. Some of God's truths are quite simple. If you cannot do great things for God, do small things in a great way. Small things can be not only beautiful but life-giving. Yield to them.

Many of us still have tragically limited understandings of grace. Unknowingly we still serve a God we think is stingy, who loves us only in proportion to how much we work for him, who is embarrassed by laughter and surprised by spontaneity. We have forgotten, or never realized, that each day is a gift—we did nothing to deserve it. We've forgotten, or refused out of arrogance to believe, that each breath is a gift, and all the work in the world won't give us more. We've forgotten, or never learned, that the mark of a believer is not only love but joy, wonder, appreciation, surprise, creativity, peace, tenacity, hope, simplicity, and even play.

A *Prayer*

England
Fifteenth Century

*God be in my head, and
in my understanding;*

*God be in my eyes, and
in my looking;*

*God be in my mouth, and
in my speaking;*

*God be in my heart, and
in my thinking;*

*God be at my end, and
in my departing.*

Telltale Marks

Karen Mains

T HE MUD MARKS SWAGGERED BOLDLY across the gold
carpet, marched around the freshly washed kitchen tile, meandered down the hall, stopped at the
bathroom sink—then ended in scattered clods of earth
on the porch and down the front steps. It all must have
happened in the space of my quick dash to a "borrowing
neighbor."

"Joel! Jo-el Da-vid!" I called. My mother-mind had
quickly assessed to which culprit the mud marks belong-
ed: the great house despoiler, Joel David Mains. Two
small figures came bounding joyously from the back
yard, their snowsuits besotted and begrimed—my son
and his pal Georgie. Georgie is five, but in stature he is
eight, causing him to lope and stumble like an adoles-
cent puppy.

"What have you been doing?" I demanded.

"Playing in the back yard," came the reply.

"No! No! What have you been doing in my house?
There's mud from front to back!" I cried.

Innocently, both boys checked their boots. All four
were huge clods of clay properly cemented to moldering
fall leaves.

"It was Georgie," maintained the ever-loyal Joel. "It was Joel," countered Georgie, a little slower on the draw.

Obviously chagrined by a mother who would make so much over such a minor incident, Joel volunteered more information. "Georgie/just/wanted/a/glass/of/water." Each word was pronounced in a separate, distinct tone, in a manner reserved for communication with the deaf, the infirm, or the half-wit.

"Well," I replied, also being deliberately distinct, "the next time Georgie wants a glass of water, tell him to/get /it/in/his/own/house." And having had the last word, I dismissed them.

Within minutes, aided by a wet rag and vacuum, I erased the telltale evidences. Glancing at the clock I discovered that two lovely hours remained before the older

children arrived home from school. Grabbing my Bible, I crept past the baby's door listening for the reassuring pattern of his breathing, then on to my very own place—a seat beneath the big window where I can see the sky, blue or gray. A little hurriedly I whispered "Here I am again, Lord. It's Karen. What have You to teach me today?"

Opening the Scripture, I continued my synoptic study of the Gospels. Certain vibrant phrases stood forth. "If, as my representatives, you give even a cup of cold water to a little child, you will surely be rewarded . . ." and "Anyone who takes care of a little child is caring for God who sent me. Your care for others is the measure of your greatness."

Shame flooded me. *Georgie just wanted a glass of water.* I bowed my heart and prayed, "Father, forgive me for caring more for clean floors and tidy schedules than for two little boys."

I can remember the time my back door opened and a grubby boot threatened to descend in ruinous contact with my kitchen floor. (Why the former tenant of the house who filled the place with eight sons would choose white tile for her decorating scheme is beyond me. All I can conclude is she must have been a wonder in courage!) Impatience welled, but an inward voice spoke first. *Be careful what you say.* Look into those eyes. Don't you see that Christ has come into your kitchen—"Anyone who takes care of a little child is caring for God who sent me."

The foot came down on the floor, and I knew at that moment this was going to be a hard discipline, this seeing Christ in those of my immediate family, in those who would leave their telltale marks over my floors and plans and life. A difficult discipline?—yes, but it is a worthy one. If I give to them but a cup of water, Christ counts it as unto Himself. I am not only called to minister to my church or to my world, but I am privileged to serve those with whom I live.

"Martha, Martha"

Helen Caswell

I am a Martha, jealous of the Marys
Of this world—the lovely, spiritual Marys
Who can listen to the words of Christ
With ears closed to the clamor of the crowd
That wants its dinner.
But someone *has to do the cooking . . .*
Doesn't someone have to do the cooking?
Maybe not. Not one of us
Is getting thinner.
I fear that it's an older wives' tale and nothing more:
That one can enter Heaven by the kitchen door.

Tough Love

Beth Werner

Sometimes we all need a dose of tough love. This is love that is not necessarily sweet and soft-worded, but love that is straightforward and honest. Sometimes, it is love that hurts, yet hurts for a healing purpose.

When my children fall and skin their knees, I clean the dirt out of the wound and apply an antiseptic solution to discourage infection. This is tough love. My children don't like it at all. They scream; they cry; they beg me not to do it, because it will hurt. But I know it must be done, and proceed.

God must often take us through cleansing experiences. They hurt. We cry. We beg God to eliminate the process from our lives. But God knows the cleansing solution that must be used to heal different parts of our lives and personalities. Then the soothing peace of His Holy Spirit covers and binds our wound as the healing process begins.

So I don't run away from God's tough love. I trust Him. I know that He will heal the hurt.

Thank You, Lord for Your tough love and Your healing Spirit.

A Song in My Heart

Anne Elver

How shall we sing the Lord's song in a strange land?—*Psalm 137:4*

Have you found yourself in a situation that made you wonder if you could still praise the Lord? I have. Our family moved to another state. A cold, snowy climate, lowered economic conditions, no familiar scenery, and longing for my family and friends left behind almost overwhelmed me.

One day I received a letter from an old friend. Reading it made me miss my former life all the more. I wept until my emotions calmed. Then I resolved to make the best of my situation. I explored various attractions in my area, discovered a good library nearby, took a few personal enrichment courses, and got involved in a Christian women's group.

Several years later, someone from my former town remarked, "The move must have agreed with you. You seem so much more confident of yourself."

Yes, God has helped me to sing in a strange land.

I thank You, Lord, for the song in my heart.

Everybody Shout Hallelujah!

Elspeth Murphy

When I think
about you, God,
I get so happy.
     It's like a beautiful
bubble inside me
blowing
          bigger
          and
          BIGGER
until it just wants to burst.

I feel like yelling,
"Come on,
you whole big world!
Tell God how
wonderful he is!"

Mother's Day

Win Couchman

Small,
I knelt
on ungiving
linoleum.
Restless,
peeking,
uneasy.

Around me
larger backsides,
bigger shoes
than mine
loomed below
bent shoulders,
bowed heads.

My mother
and mother's mother
and assorted saints
of their generations
were kneeling.

Fifty years
and more
have gone.
And I remember:
They prayed.